THE HOUND OF THE BASKERVILLES

by
Sir Arthur Conan Doyle

Teacher Guide

Written by
Joan F. Langham

> **Note**
> The Signet Classic paperback version of the novel, © 2001, was used to prepare this guide. Page references may differ in other editions.
> Novel ISBN: 0-451-52801-8
>
> **Please note:** Please assess the appropriateness of this book for the age level and maturity of your students prior to reading and discussing it with them.

ISBN 1-58130-855-8
Copyright infringement is a violation of Federal Law.

© 2005 by Novel Units, Inc., Bulverde, Texas. All rights reserved. No part of this publication may be reproduced, translated, stored in a retrieval system, or transmitted in any way or by any means (electronic, mechanical, photocopying, recording, or otherwise) without prior written permission from Novel Units, Inc.

Photocopying of student worksheets by a classroom teacher at a non-profit school who has purchased this publication for his/her own class is permissible. Reproduction of any part of this publication for an entire school or for a school system, by for-profit institutions and tutoring centers, or for commercial sale is strictly prohibited.

Novel Units is a registered trademark of Novel Units, Inc. Printed in the United States of America.

To order, contact your local school supply store, or—
Novel Units, Inc.
P.O. Box 97
Bulverde, TX 78163-0097

Web site: www.educyberstor.com

Lori Mammen, Editorial Director
Andrea M. Harris, Production Manager/Production Specialist
Suzanne K. Mammen, Curriculum Specialist
Heather Johnson, Product Development Specialist
Vicky Rainwater, Curriculum Specialist
Jill Reed, Product Development Specialist
Nancy Smith, Product Development Specialist
Adrienne Speer, Production Specialist
Lenella Meister, Production Specialist

Table of Contents

Summary 3

Characters 3

About the Author 4

Initiating Activities 5

Vocabulary Activities 5

Five Sections 15
   Each section contains: Summary, Vocabulary,
   Discussion Questions, and Supplementary Activities

Post-reading Discussion Questions 23

Post-reading Extension Activities 24

Assessment 25

Scoring Rubric 26

Glossary 27

Skills and Strategies

Art
Poster, book jacket, collage, illustration

Comprehension
Identifying clues, creative and critical thinking, predicting, interpreting, evaluation, observation

Thinking
Research, compare/contrast, analysis, problem solving, supporting details, sequencing, deduction

Writing
Letter, diary, essay, journal, poem, description, paraphrase, biography

Literary Elements
Style, point of view, theme, Gothicism, foil, setting, imagery, characterization

Listening/Speaking
Discussion, personal experiences, oral reports

Genre: mystery

Setting: London and Devonshire (Dartmoor); 1889

Point of View: first-person participant

Narrator: Dr. Watson

Themes: good vs. evil, natural vs. supernatural, reality vs. fantasy

Conflict: person vs. person

Protagonists: Sherlock Holmes, Dr. Watson

Antagonists: the hound, Stapleton

Tone: mysterious, suspenseful

Date of Publication: Published in monthly installments in *The Strand Mystery Magazine* (August 1901–April 1902) with illustrations; book was published on March 25, 1902

Summary

The great detective Sherlock Holmes is asked to solve the mystery of the death of Sir Charles Baskerville. The legend of the Hound of the Baskervilles declares that there is a curse on the family because of Sir Hugo Baskerville's violence toward a yeoman's daughter years before. A great hound hovered over Sir Hugo's dead body, and many believe the curse of the hound continues to pursue the Baskerville family. Sir Charles' heir, Sir Henry Baskerville, receives a warning in a cryptic note telling him not to go onto the moor. Holmes sends his assistant, Dr. Watson, to live at Baskerville Hall with Sir Henry and investigate the source of the warning. Holmes remains in London, receiving letters from Dr. Watson reciting the events in Devonshire at the hall and on the moor. He tells Holmes of the Barrymores' strange activities at night, the tension between Mr. Stapleton and his sister, Sir Henry's romantic interest, the criminal Selden's relationship to the Barrymores, the stranger on the moor, and the howling of the hound. The interweaving of the Stapletons, the Barrymores, Dr. Mortimer, Sir Henry, Frankland, Laura Lyons, and Selden add to the complexity of the mystery. Holmes himself secretly comes to the moor and observes various events. Ultimately, Holmes pronounces Stapleton as the murderer and resolves all the loose ends of the mystery.

Characters

Sherlock Holmes: brilliant and renowned British detective; hired to discover what really happened to Sir Charles Baskerville

Dr. Watson: assistant to Sherlock Holmes; goes to Dartmoor to observe and report findings

Dr. Mortimer: doctor from Devonshire; friend of Sir Charles Baskerville; brings the manuscript and story of the hound to Sherlock Holmes and Watson

Sir Hugo Baskerville: Baskerville ancestor whose wicked and wanton ways led to the curse on the Baskerville family

Sir Charles Baskerville: kind but superstitious Baskerville heir who dies of heart failure after seeing the hound on the moor

Sir Henry Baskerville: Baskerville heir who arrives from Canada to take up his position at Baskerville Hall

John and Eliza Barrymore: Sir Charles' butler and maid; the last of five generations of servants in Baskerville Hall

Selden: convict; Mrs. Barrymore's brother

Jack Stapleton: clandestine relative of Sir Charles Baskerville; resident of the moor; a naturalist

Miss Beryl Stapleton: Stapleton's beautiful, elegant, but mysterious sister; love interest of Sir Henry; later discovered to be Stapleton's wife

Laura Lyons: woman seeking Sir Charles' help in getting a divorce so she can marry Stapleton; used as a pawn by Stapleton

Lestrade: policeman from London; arrives to help apprehend Stapleton

About the Author

Personal: Born May 22, 1859, to Mary and Charles Altamont Doyle, Arthur Ignatius Conan Doyle was one of ten children. Doyle was educated at home and in local schools and was eventually put in the Jesuit Preparatory School of Hodder in Lancashire at the age of nine; later he went to Stonyhurst. Although a bright and gifted student, he did not have many friends. He spent most of his time writing letters to his mother and stories to entertain his classmates. At the age of 16, he traveled to Austria to study. There, his love of reading was nourished by authors such as Edgar Allan Poe and Jules Verne. Eventually, he attended Edinburgh Medical School. In 1881, at the age of 22, he received a bachelor of medicine and a master of surgery. With his wife Louisa, whom he married in 1884, Doyle set up practice as a surgeon in Portsmouth, England. He had very few patients and spent his free time writing. He quit his practice to work as a professional author. After his first wife died, he married again and had three children. During World War I, his eldest son, two nephews, two brothers-in-law, and a brother were killed. These deaths led Doyle into a life of spiritualism, to which he was devoted until he died from heart disease on July 7, 1930.

Professional: Sir Arthur Conan Doyle received a knightship from King Edward VII for working in and writing about the Boer War. He did not want to accept the knightship; however, his mother insisted that he should not insult the king. His greatest writing contribution was the famous detective Sherlock Holmes, who first appeared in "The Study in Scarlet" in 1887. His second story, "The Sign of the Four," gained Doyle fame. He wrote a series of short stories entitled *The Adventures of Sherlock Holmes*. Over 60 stories about Sherlock Holmes appeared from 1887–1927. In addition to detective stories and novels, Doyle wrote historical novels, pamphlets, and spiritualist works.

Initiating Activities

1. Invite a detective to class to tell the students about his work. Have students ask any questions that they feel will help them as they read *The Hound of the Baskervilles*.

2. Read one of Sir Arthur Conan Doyle's short stories to the class. Discuss the fictional elements: setting, atmosphere, point of view, tone, conflict, protagonist, antagonist, climax, and resolution.

3. Research and answer the following questions:
    a. In what country is *The Hound of the Baskervilles* set?
    b. In what era was this novel written?
    c. From where does the title come?
    d. Where do Sherlock Holmes and Dr. Watson live?
    e. What elements form a detective story?
    f. What are *gothic* elements?
    g. What is the difference between a detective story and a horror story?
    h. Who are some other famous mystery writers?

4. Locate the Devonshire area on a map of England. Research the geographical terrain, noting especially the tors, downs, and moors.

5. Complete the graphic on page 6 of this guide.

Vocabulary Activities

1. Choose nine words from the glossary on pages 27–28 of this guide. Place these words on the chalkboard in Tic-Tac-Toe form. Divide students into two teams and have each team take turns choosing a square. In order to win their square, the team must give the correct definition, give one synonym of the word, or use the word correctly in a sentence. Continue until one team completes a Tic-Tac-Toe.

2. Have students complete Word Maps (see page 7 of this guide) for specified vocabulary words.

3. Encourage students to create their own glossary of difficult or challenging words they encounter while reading the novel.

Getting the "Lay of the Land"

Directions: Prepare for reading by answering the following short-answer questions.

1. Who is the author?

   _____

2. What does the title suggest to you about the book?

   _____
   _____
   _____
   _____

3. When was the book first copyrighted?

   _____

4. How many pages are there in the book?

   _____

5. Look at the front cover. What adjectives describe the illustration? Do you think these will also describe the story?

   _____
   _____
   _____
   _____
   _____

6. Read the back cover. List items from the blurb that indicate the novel will be a mystery.

   _____
   _____
   _____
   _____

Word Map

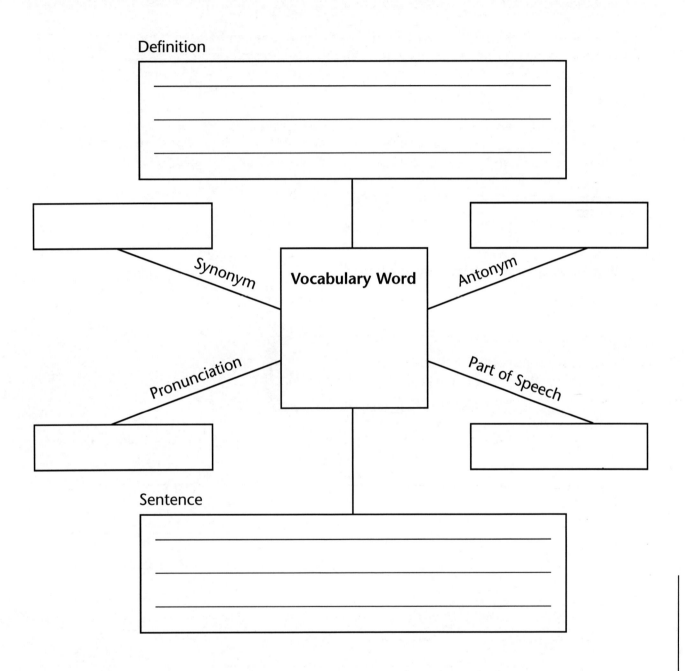

Using Predictions

We all make predictions as we read—little guesses about what will happen next, how a conflict will be resolved, which details will be important to the plot, which details will help fill in our sense of a character. Students should be encouraged to predict, to make sensible guesses as they read the novel.

As students work on their predictions, these discussion questions can be used to guide them: What are some of the ways to predict? What is the process of a sophisticated reader's thinking and predicting? What clues does an author give to help us make predictions? Why are some predictions more likely to be accurate than others?

Create a chart for recording predictions. This could either be an individual or class activity. As each subsequent chapter is discussed, students can review and correct their previous predictions about plot and characters as necessary.

- Use the facts and ideas the author gives.
- Use your own prior knowledge.
- Apply any new information (i.e., from class discussion) that may cause you to change your mind.

Predictions
_____
_____
_____
_____

Prediction Chart

What characters have we met so far?	What is the conflict in the story?	What are your predictions?	Why did you make these predictions?

Story Map

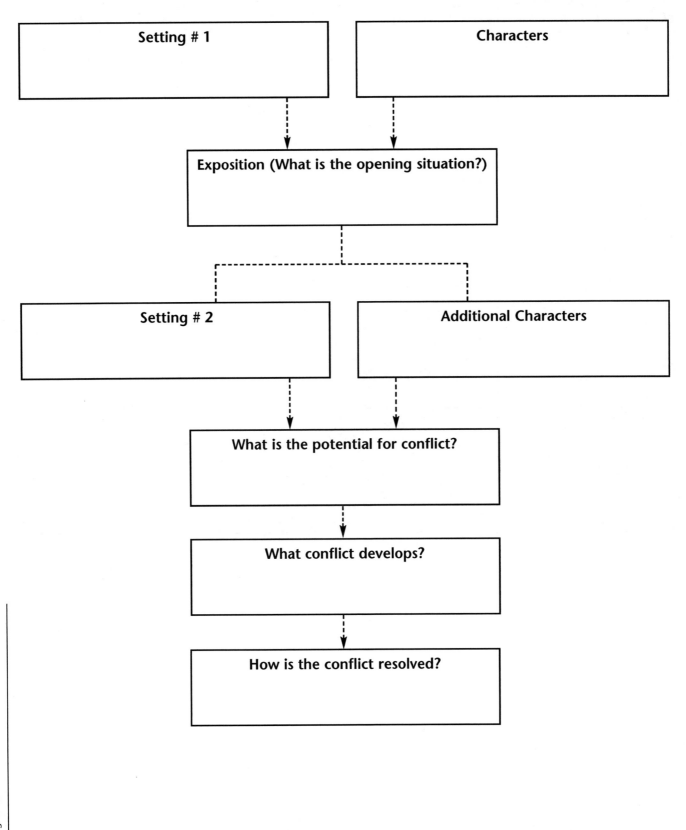

Using Character Attribute Webs

Character attribute webs are simply a visual representation of a character from the novel. They provide a systematic way for students to organize and recap the information they have about a particular character. Attribute webs may be used after reading the novel to recapitulate information about a particular character, or completed gradually as information unfolds. They may be completed individually or as a group project.

One type of character attribute web uses these divisions:

- How a character acts and feels. (How does the character act? How do you think the character feels? How would you feel if this happened to you?)

- How a character looks. (Close your eyes and picture the character. Describe him/her.)

- Where a character lives. (Where and when does the character live?)

- How others feel about the character. (How does another specific character feel about the character?)

In group discussion about the characters described in student attribute webs, the teacher can ask for backup proof from the novel. Inferential thinking can be included in the discussion.

Character Web

Directions: Complete the attribute web below.

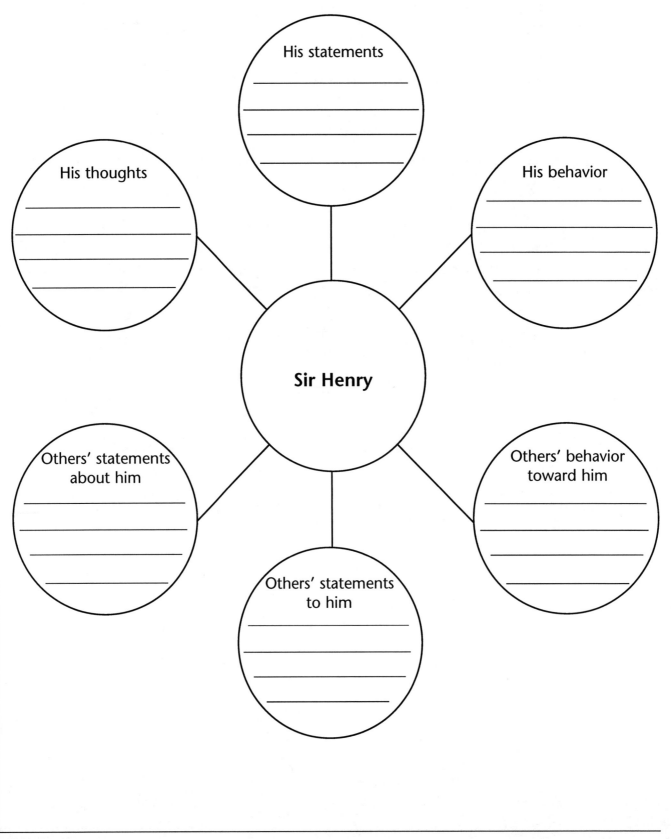

Character Attribute Web

Directions: The attribute web below will help you gather clues the author provides about a character in the novel. Fill in the blanks with words and phrases that tell how the character acts and looks, as well as what the character says and feels.

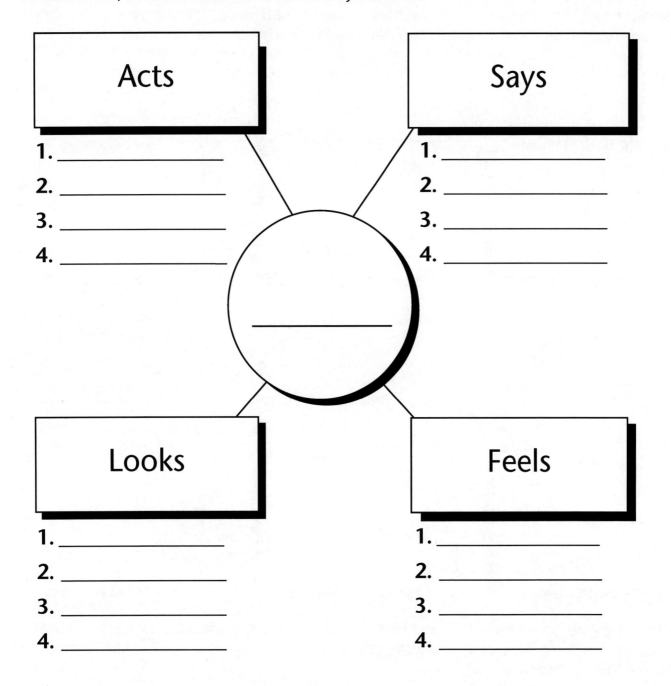

Understanding Values

Values represent people's beliefs about what is important, good, or worthwhile. For example, most families value spending time together.

Directions: Think about the following characters from *The Hound of the Baskervilles* and the values they exhibit. What do they value? What beliefs do they have about what is important, good, or worthwhile? On the chart below, list each character's three most important values, from most important to least. Be prepared to share your lists during a class discussion.

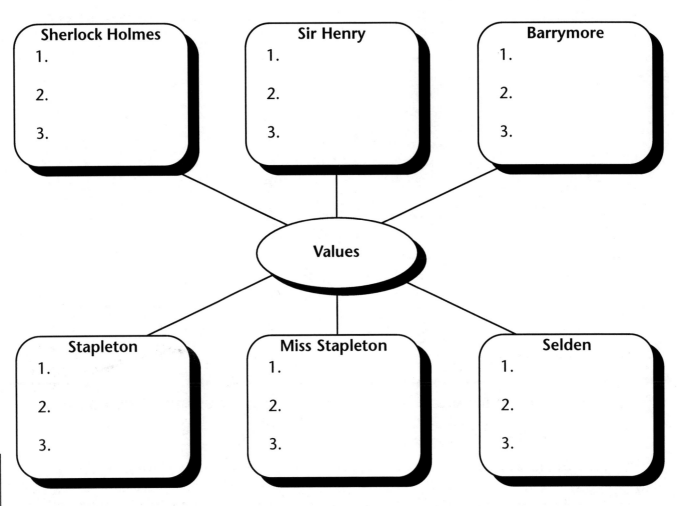

After you have finished the chart and participated in the class discussion, think about which character seems to have values most like your own. Write a paragraph that explains why you chose this character.

Chapters 1–3, pp. 9–45

The reader is introduced to Sherlock Holmes and Dr. Watson. They are using logical reasoning to discover facts about a man who has left his cane at Holmes' office. Eventually, Dr. Mortimer arrives to see the detective, and Holmes and Watson discover most of their deductions are accurate. Dr. Mortimer has a manuscript containing the history of Sir Hugo Baskerville and the beginning of the legend of the Hound of the Baskervilles, the horrific dog that is allegedly haunting the Baskerville family. Sir Charles Baskerville's tragic death from heart failure is described, and Holmes offers his hypotheses of the scene.

Vocabulary

ferrule (10)
erroneous (11)
incredulously (13)
astutely (14)
anthropological (16)
wanton (21)
leagues (22)
anon (23)
bemused (23)
*roysterers (24)
scion (26)
prosaic (28)
chimerical (31)
diabolical (37)
immaculate (41)
*archaic spelling

Discussion Questions

1. Analyze the story found in the manuscript that Dr. Mortimer brings to Sherlock Holmes. *(In the 17th century, Sir Hugo Baskerville, a wealthy landowner in England, had a reputation for being wild and immoral. He also had a cruel side to him. Unfortunately, he lusted for one of the nearby peasant girls who lived on his land. She rejected him, so he kidnapped her and brought her to his manor. After much drinking with his friends, he decided to take some food and drink to her. When he arrived in her apartment, he found that she had climbed down the ivy and had run back home. Furious, Sir Hugo retrieved his horse and hounds to pursue her. His friends followed. They found the maiden dead from fright and exhaustion. Sir Hugo was lying next to her, having been killed by a huge, beastly hound. This event was the beginning of the legend known as the Hound of the Baskervilles. pp. 21–25)*

2. Explain why the content of the manuscript is important to the story. *(The manuscript lays the foundation for the entire novel: a wealthy family with land, a curse on the family, a huge dog, the wanton and cruel character that runs in the family, and a shadow that falls on future generations. It prepares the reader for the mystery ahead by creating questions in the reader's mind. pp. 21–25)*

3. Describe Sir Charles Baskerville. *(Sir Charles is a gentleman who came from a long line of gentry. He is a widower who lives a simple life at his ancestral home—Baskerville Hall. Known for having a weak heart, he has a reputation for kindness, amiability, and generosity. Earning money abroad, he has brought his fortune back to England and has used it to improve his home- and county-groups [local and county charities]. Many individuals have benefited from his wealth. Sir Charles was thinking of running for Parliament before he died. pp. 26, 27, 38)*

4. What skills make Sherlock Homes an expert detective? *(excellent thinker, observant, knowledgeable, thorough, asks in-depth questions, logical, self-confident, a bit arrogant about his ability, has built a reputation of being the best, ability to sort and evaluate, intense concentration, excellent at deduction and inference, pp. 9–17, 40–43)*

5. Why doesn't Holmes give credence to the supernatural nature of the Hound of the Baskervilles? *(Holmes is a true Victorian—a man of science. In fact, he considers himself a "scientific expert." A supernatural hound would be totally against his character and thinking because he deals in the world of reality. He delves into unsolved cases and traces facts rather than fantasy. The few facts he knows about Sir Charles' death [footprint, howling, and sightings] point to a real animal as far as he is concerned. He comments that "a devil with merely local powers…would be too inconceivable a thing." pp. 35–39)*

6. Contrast Sir Hugo and Sir Charles Baskerville. *(Sir Hugo: wealthy, landed gentry, mean, oppressive, arrogant, "wild," "profane," "godless," "wanton and cruel humor," had an "evil name," kidnapper, reveler, curser, said he would give his "soul to the Powers of Evil"; Sir Charles: wealthy, talented businessman, kind, generous, compassionate, good neighbor, a gentleman, lived simply, pp. 21–25, 26–28)*

7. Why do you think Sir Charles Baskerville was waiting in the alley? Why did he go beyond the gate when he did not usually do so? *(Answers will vary.)*

8. Discuss the effectiveness of a novel written in first-person participant. *(First person enables the reader to take part in the experiences of the narrator [Dr. Watson]. The reader knows what is occurring each minute in clear detail. The excitement and tension of the mystery is better conveyed by a first-person narrator and gives the reader the feeling that he is being spoken to directly. First person brings the reader close to the narrator, making the action more alive and real.)*

Supplementary Activities

1. Begin a Prediction Chart (see pages 8–9 of this guide) to use as you read the novel.

2. Begin the Story Map on page 10 of this guide.

3. Elements within a story that are scary, supernatural, or lend mystery to a story are often known as gothic elements. Make a list of gothic elements or language as you read *The Hound of the Baskervilles*.

4. Sherlock Holmes states, "The world is full of obvious things which nobody by any chance ever observes" (p. 41). In 2–3 paragraphs, explain this quotation and give examples of the "obvious things" to which Holmes may have been referring.

Chapters 4–6, pp. 46–91

Sir Henry Baskerville arrives from Canada and meets Dr. Mortimer, Sherlock Holmes, and Watson. Sir Henry has received a cryptic note, warning him against going onto the moor. Also, while he is at the hotel, a new brown boot is stolen from him. Holmes and Watson know that Sir Henry is being followed. Oddly, Sir Henry discovers his new boot in his room; however, an old black boot disappears soon after. Holmes decides to send Watson to watch over Sir Henry at Baskerville Hall. As they arrive in Devonshire, Sir Henry's home appears to be a dark, dreary, and drab residence. Late that night, Watson hears the heart-wrenching crying of a woman.

Discussion Questions

1. Describe Sir Henry Baskerville. *(Sir Henry is a young man about 30 years old. He is stocky, with thick, black eyebrows and a strong-looking face. His dark eyes are small but alert at all times, and his temper is evident, but his manner represents that of a gentleman. He appears to have spent much of his life outdoors. He is not frightened by the legend of his family's curse, nor by the person who is attempting to scare him away from Baskerville Hall. pp. 46–56)*

2. Analyze Chapter 5, entitled "Three Broken Threads." *(The three threads are clues that Holmes follows. The first thread refers to the whereabouts of Mr. Barrymore, a servant in Baskerville Hall. Holmes sends a telegram to Barrymore in order to determine if he is at home or in London. The second thread is the origin of the paper used in the note received by Sir Henry. But after sending a young boy to visit many hotels and dig through trashcans, Holmes does not find anything helpful. The third thread is identifying the spy in the cab, but the spy outwits Holmes by telling the cabman that his name is Sherlock Holmes. pp. 61, 63–77)*

Vocabulary
pugnacious (46)
foolscap (47)
bourgeois (50)
singular (53)
languid (57)
hansom (58)
malevolent (59)
articulate (65)
entailed (69)
inexplicable (72)
toff (76)
imprudent (80)
bracken (83)
equestrian (83)
atrocious (84)
surmounted (85)
crenellated (86)
mullioned (86)
balustraded (89)
resonant (90)

3. How does Baskerville Hall support the atmosphere of suspense and mystery already set by the moor? *(The author describes Baskerville Hall from the avenue leading up to the interior by using vocabulary denoting darkness and gloom—supporting the eerie atmosphere set by the moor outside. The avenue up to the house is called "sombre," and the house itself looks "like a ghost." The house is large, covered with ivy towers and turrets, "a ruin of black granite," and "heavy mullioned windows." Black smoke pours from the chimney. The rooms are large and dark, with "age-blackened oak" and an old fireplace. The dining hall is also a place of gloom, having "a smoke-darkened ceiling" and "a dim line of" ancestral pictures along the wall with "black beams." Sir Henry comments, "…it isn't a very cheerful place." Watson states that a "deathly silence lay upon the old house." The description of the hall supports the overall tone of the novel. pp. 85–91)*

4. What is outstanding about Doyle's writing to this point? *(Answers will vary. Suggestions: Doyle sets the scene for the entire novel by putting the legend in the manuscript. Doyle combines gothic and dreary atmospheres on the moor and at Baskerville Hall. He uses appropriate descriptive language to set the scene. Doyle begins building suspense with a cryptic note and lost boots, adds interesting characters such as Sir Henry, Sir Charles, Barrymore, and the bearded man, and creates a story the reader wants to continue reading.)*

5. Why is Dr. Watson the perfect narrator for the novel? *(Answers will vary. Suggestions: The reader can relate to Watson because he is a common man and not an expert detective like Holmes. Watson does not always get things right, and his theories are often wrong, but he tries very hard to impress Sherlock Holmes. Watson seems to be a congenial, social gentleman, contrasting sharply with the arrogant and reclusive Holmes. He has admirable qualities, such as bravery and loyalty, making him more attractive for the reader to "listen to" as he tells about their adventures.)*

6. **Prediction:** Who is the woman sobbing late at night at Baskerville Hall?

Supplementary Activities

1. Analyze Sir Henry Baskerville using the Character Web on pages 11–12 of this guide.
2. Write a letter to Sherlock Holmes from Dr. Watson, telling him what you have discovered during your stay at Baskerville Hall.
3. Research the morals and manners of the Victorian Era. Present your findings to the class in an oral report.
4. Make an illustration of the Hound of the Baskervilles as it has been described so far in the novel.

Chapters 7–9, pp. 92–144

Sir Henry believes Barrymore's wife is the woman crying at night. Dr. Watson suspects that Mr. Barrymore wants to inherit the Baskerville fortune and is responsible for the harassment of Sir Henry in London. While out on the moor, Watson meets Mr. Stapleton, a naturalist. They discuss the moor and the legend of the hound. As they walk, Stapleton's beautiful sister comes along. Thinking Watson is Sir Henry, she warns him to leave Baskerville Hall. Watson notices the strained relationship between Mr. and Miss Stapleton. Eventually, Sir Henry becomes romantically interested in Miss Stapleton, but her brother dislikes this show of interest. Mr. Barrymore is caught signaling Selden, a criminal on the moor, who turns out to be Mrs. Barrymore's brother. As Watson and Sir Henry attempt to capture the criminal, they hear the howling of a great hound and see a dark figure silhouetted against the sky.

Vocabulary

- pallid (93)
- propitious (94)
- ruse (95)
- placid (98)
- wary (98)
- undulating (99)
- mottled (101)
- wizened (106)
- monoliths (112)
- antiquarian (112)
- disapprobation (115)
- onerous (115)
- choleric (116)
- effigy (117)
- stealthy (119)
- furtive (119)
- peremptory (127)
- unmitigated (137)
- inscrutable (144)

Discussion Questions

1. What careful observations does Watson make about Mr. and Miss Stapleton's relationship? *(Watson notices the contrast in their appearance. Mr. Stapleton is "neutral tinted, with light hair and gray eyes." Miss Stapleton is an elegant, beautiful brunette with dark eyes. There is also a difference in their approach to Sir Henry. Miss Stapleton warns Watson against going onto the moor, obviously against her brother's wishes. Watson notes a strained, tense feeling passing between them. When Mr. Stapleton comments that his sister and he are happy on the moor, she answers that yes, she is happy, but Watson says, "…there was no ring of conviction in her words." Soon after, she catches Watson on the moor to apologize and to again warn him. Once more, she mentions her brother's displeasure with her warning Sir Henry. He notices the strong influence Stapleton has on his sister, as she glances at him for approval when they talk to company. Watson notices Stapleton's disapproval of Sir Henry's attention to his sister, even though she does not seem to mind it. Watson decides that the siblings have very different motives in everything they say or do. pp. 104–106, 114–115)*

2. Why are Barrymore, his wife, and the criminal on the moor effective characters in the novel? *(The Barrymores provide the story with two more people who may want to harm Sir Henry and the Baskerville family, adding to the difficulty of Sherlock Holmes' task. Initially, the Barrymores say that they are leaving Sir Henry's service. The question remains as to their motives for wanting to leave. Barrymore lies about his wife's crying at night for no apparent reason. Their personalities are strange, and they behave oddly at night. There is a haunting quality about them. They add suspense and mystery to the novel. Since they are the previous baronet's servants, it seems they know more than they are disclosing. The criminal on the moor adds danger to the story. He is an escaped murderer, and no one knows what he is capable of. pp. 93–94, 131–144)*

3. What part, if any, will the Grimpen Mire play in solving the mystery? *(Answers will vary. Suggestions: It will probably be important because Stapleton describes it in detail to Watson. The fact that ponies can be swallowed up in the Mire is probably another piece of the puzzle, and Stapleton takes time to tell the entire gruesome tale. p. 100)*

4. Based on what you have read so far, who are the possible suspects in the plot to harm Sir Henry Baskerville? *(Answers will vary.)*

5. Examine Dr. Watson's reports to Sherlock Homes. Why hasn't Holmes come to Baskerville Hall, even after reading Watson's intriguing reports? *(Watson sends Holmes information on all proceedings at the hall, relevant or not. He describes people, places, and events that seem to provide clues to the Baskervilles' curse, hoping that Holmes can use this information to solve the mystery. He is concerned for Sir Henry's safety, and he tells Sherlock Holmes so. Answers will vary. pp. 111–144)*

6. **Prediction:** Who is the dark stranger on the moor?

Supplementary Activities

1. Create a collage of the strange things Dr. Watson has witnessed thus far, e.g., a woman sobbing, Mr. and Miss Stapleton, the dark figure on the moor, etc.

2. Write a diary entry as if you were Watson, giving your impressions of the events since your arrival at Baskerville Hall.

3. Read a horror or mystery tale by Edgar Allan Poe. For example, "The Murders in the Rue Morgue," "The Purloined Letter," "The Tell-Tale Heart," "The Pit and the Pendulum," "The Masque of the Red Death," or "The Cask of Amontillado."

4. Create a short "mystery" for the class to solve. For example:

   Mystery: Sally has 15 cents in her pocket. She has 2 coins, and one of them is not a nickel. What two coins does Sally have in her pocket?

   Answer: A dime and a nickel. ONE of the coins is NOT a nickel, but one IS a nickel.

Chapters 10–12, pp. 145–193

Watson discovers that the woman Sir Charles Baskerville was waiting for before his death is Laura Lyons. He also discovers that the stranger on the moor is Sherlock Holmes, who has been secretly observing the events the entire time. A man is killed on the moor, and Holmes and Watson think it is Sir Henry. Holmes and Watson rush to the man, only to discover that the victim is Selden, wearing Sir Henry's clothes. Holmes pronounces Stapleton as the man trying to harm Sir Henry, but without proof, he cannot charge him. Stapleton arrives and realizes the dead man is Selden, not Sir Henry. Holmes does not hint that he believes Stapleton is the murderer of both Sir Charles and Selden.

Discussion Questions

1. Discuss possible answers to the questions posed by Watson, "…where could such a hound lie concealed, where did it get its food, where did it come from, how is it that no one saw it by day?" *(Answers will vary. pp. 146–147)*

2. Why is Barrymore's confession of finding the letter sent to Sir Charles by "L.L." important to the case? Why did Barrymore keep this information from Dr. Watson and Sir Henry? *(The letter reveals the reason for Sir Charles' waiting in the alley at night—he was meeting a woman. Dr. Watson is certain that if they can discover the identity of "L.L." they will determine how and why Sir Charles died. Barrymore was frightened that if he revealed the letter's existence, his family and Sir Charles' good reputation would be in jeopardy. pp. 150–151)*

Vocabulary

sodden (153)
morass (153)
equivocal (155)
almoner (162)
reticent (166)
roughshod (168)
incredulity (170)
solicitations (172)
dilapidated (173)
pannikin (174)
malignant (175)
tenacity (178)
irrevocable (188)
precipitous (188)
paroxysm (189)

3. How does Watson discover that the stranger on the moor is really Sherlock Holmes? *(Mr. Frankland tells him that a young boy is bringing food to the stranger every night. Watson follows the boy onto the moor one night and comes upon the stranger's living area. He finds a written message that reveals the stranger is watching him, not Sir Henry. Watson waits for the stranger's return, and upon hearing the man's voice, realizes it is Holmes. pp. 170–176)*

4. Why hasn't Holmes revealed his identity until now? *(Answers will vary. Suggestions: Holmes claims that he did not want Watson to know he was there because then he would have had to comfort and reassure Watson. Holmes, in his usual arrogant manner, does not give Watson credit for being able to conduct himself successfully without Holmes' assistance. Holmes wanted to stay in the shadows so that he could witness the events and have time to produce a solution to the mystery. p. 180)*

5. What clues does Holmes reveal to Watson about the case involving Sir Henry Baskerville? *(Holmes tells Watson that Miss Stapleton is actually Stapleton's wife, not his sister. Laura Lyons, the woman who wrote the note to Sir Charles, was asking for his help in divorcing her husband. Stapleton had promised her that he would marry her if she did so. Stapleton was the man who followed Sir Henry, Holmes, and Watson in London. Holmes knows that Stapleton is the culprit, but he cannot yet prove it. pp. 182–184)*

6. Why does the hound pursue and kill Selden on the moor? *(Barrymore gave Selden some of Sir Henry's clothes, and Selden was walking on the moor. The hound had been introduced to Sir Henry's scent by the stolen boots from London, and it followed the scent on Sir Henry's clothes. p. 189)*

7. Analyze Stapleton's reaction to seeing that the dead man on the moor is Selden, not Sir Henry. *(Answers will vary. Suggestions: Stapleton is obviously surprised, but he conceals his guilt well. He asks many questions, and he admits to inviting Sir Henry to his house. pp. 190–193)*

8. What is Holmes' purpose in telling Stapleton that he and Dr. Watson are returning to London when, in fact, they are not? *(Holmes hopes that if Stapleton believes they are gone, he will make an attempt on Sir Henry's life, therefore allowing Holmes to catch him in the act. p. 192)*

9. **Prediction:** Why does Stapleton want to kill Sir Henry?

Supplementary Activities

1. Write an acrostic using the word MYSTERY.

2. Read Edgar Allan Poe's "The Fall of the House of Usher." Compare and contrast the cursed Usher and Baskerville families. Write a 2–3 paragraph essay explaining your ideas.

3. Below are generic phrases found in *The Hound of the Baskervilles* that might appear in any mystery novel. Working with a partner, write a brief scene from an imaginary novel using one of the phrases. Read your scene aloud. If possible, combine all the scenes and perform a class skit.

    a. Consider the long sequence of incidents which have all pointed to some sinister influence which is at work around us. (p. 146)

b. I swear that another day shall not have passed before I have done all that man can do to reach the heart of the mystery. (p. 158)

c. "But why a rendezvous in the garden instead of a visit to the house?" (p. 164)

d. With tingling nerves but a fixed purpose, I sat in the dark recess…and waited with sombre patience… (p. 175)

e. "I am giving you some information…in return for all that you have given me." (p. 182)

Chapters 13–15, pp. 194–240

Holmes reveals to Watson that Stapleton is actually a Baskerville, hoping to inherit the family's fortune. He is Sir Charles' nephew, born to a Baskerville who fled the country and changed his name. Holmes devises a plan to capture Stapleton, although he does not reveal the plan in its entirety to anyone. Holmes convinces Sir Henry to walk home across the moor after leaving Stapleton's house. He also enlists the help of a police officer named Lestrade and reveals Miss Stapleton's identity to Laura Lyons. After hearing of Stapleton's deception, Ms. Lyons tells Holmes that it was Stapleton's idea to send the letter to Sir Charles, asking for money to help with her divorce, and that she had no idea it would result in his death. Holmes, Watson, and Lestrade watch Sir Henry walk across the moor and witness the legendary hound appear. The hound chases Sir Henry, but Holmes and Watson shoot it before it can harm him. They briefly attempt to calm Sir Henry before pursuing Stapleton. However, Stapleton meets his death in the Grimpen Mire before he can be apprehended. Holmes discovers that Miss Stapleton was tied up in the house so that she would be unable to warn Sir Henry. Soon after, they discover the place where Stapleton kept the hound. The mystery of the Hound of the Baskervilles is solved.

Vocabulary

connoisseur (199)
implicitly (202)
serrated (214)
exultant (216)
hackles (216)
mastiff (217)
doddering (219)
swathed (220)
dupe (221)
quagmires (222)
miasmatic (222)
barrister (227)
purloined (228)
finesse (230)
specious (231)
expedient (233)
audacity (233)
elucidate (234)

Discussion Questions

1. Sherlock Holmes says that he and Dr. Watson have never met "a foeman more worthy of our steel" (p. 194) than Stapleton. Discuss why Stapleton is a worthy adversary for Holmes' expert ability. *(Stapleton is like Holmes himself—clever, confident, intelligent, determined, shrewd, and arrogant. Because of his illusion of kindness, his innocent demeanor, and his intelligence, he is a challenge for Holmes. Holmes must employ a higher level of thinking in order to outsmart a man such as Stapleton.)*

2. Now that Stapleton has been identified as the murderer, examine clues from the story that foreshadowed his guilt. *(It is obvious he has studied the moor and knows it well. He explains the Grimpen Mire and dangers on the moor in detail. Stapleton also knows about the legendary hound and the curse on the Baskervilles. Finally, he knows about Sir Charles' heart problem. When Stapleton speaks of the hound, Watson observes, "He spoke with a smile, but I seemed to read in his eyes that he took the matter more seriously" [p. 97]. Stapleton also seems to be overly concerned about Sir Henry Baskerville throughout the story. When asked about certain things involving Holmes' case, Stapleton feigns ignorance.)*

3. Why does Holmes feel that it is necessary to tell Laura Lyons the truth about Stapleton? *(He hopes that Ms. Lyons will disclose more information about the night Sir Charles died after she discovers that Stapleton deceived her. His hopes are realized, and Ms. Lyons gives Holmes the final evidence of Stapleton's guilt. pp. 205–208)*

4. Describe the Hound of the Baskervilles. How did it acquire such an appearance? *(The hound is an enormous, coal-black creature with glowing eyes. Fire comes from its mouth, and its body appears to be outlined in flickering flames. The hound emits savage roars, baring its gigantic jaws as it attacks. It is a beast hideous enough to scare a man to death without ever having to wound him. Stapleton covered the hound in a phosphorous mixture, which made the creature's body glow and appear to be on fire. He kept the hound chained to ensure its savage nature. pp. 216–218, 224)*

5. How do the women in the novel contribute to the mystery? *(Answers will vary. The women add an edge that would not exist if they were absent. The Victorian woman was very much a lady, but dominated by the male members of the family. Therefore, Stapleton is able to manipulate both his wife and Laura Lyons. Miss Stapleton is used as a pawn to lure Sir Henry to the house, and Ms. Lyons is used to draw Sir Charles outside to the moor. Interestingly though, each woman turns on Stapleton when they discover his deceptive and evil nature. Mrs. Barrymore is perhaps the weakest of the female characters in the novel; however, she does supply the reader with another suspect in the plot against the Baskervilles. throughout)*

Supplementary Activities

1. Create a book jacket that would entice someone to read *The Hound of the Baskervilles*.

2. List descriptive words and phrases that prepare the reader for the sudden and terrifying appearance of the hound (see pages 214–217).

3. Do one of the following: (a) Create an illustration of the hound (b) Write a police report of Stapleton's death (c) Write a synopsis of the case from Dr. Watson's viewpoint.

Post-reading Discussion Questions

1. Does Sherlock Holmes live up to his reputation as an expert detective? Explain why or why not.

2. Why do you think *The Hound of the Baskervilles* has remained a classic for over 100 years?

3. Analyze Dr. Watson and Sherlock Holmes' friendship. Why do you suppose this friendship is successful?

4. Why do you think readers enjoy mysteries, especially murder mysteries?

5. What are some differences between a mystery (e.g., Sir Arthur Conan Doyle) and a horror story (e.g., Edgar Allan Poe)?

6. Explain the contrast between the Victorian middle class (Sherlock Holmes, Dr. Watson) and the peasant class (Devonshire villagers, the Barrymores). Consider education, occupations, lifestyle, and belief in the supernatural.

7. Why do authors such as Doyle, the Brontës, Agatha Christie, and Thomas Hardy frequently use the English moors as a setting for their novels?

8. A *foil* is a character that by contrast emphasizes the distinctive characteristics of another character. How does Watson act as a successful foil to Holmes? How does the convict act as a foil to Stapleton?

9. Describe how Doyle manages to create a realistic, believable novel even while writing about a giant hound that haunts a family.

Post-reading Extension Activities

Art

1. Create a poster advertising *The Hound of the Baskervilles* as a movie or TV show.
2. Design a collage with images of significant items from the novel: cane, hound, moor, ancestral home, etc.

History

3. Research historical mysteries, such as Stonehenge, the building of the Great Pyramids, and the Bermuda Triangle.
4. Research the landmarks on the moor as mentioned in the novel.

Further Reading

5. Locate other novels and short stories with similar settings to *The Hound of the Baskervilles*. Choose one to read and create a report for the class.
6. Read another of Sir Arthur Conan Doyle's Sherlock Holmes stories.

Research

7. Research the famous Dr. Moriarty created by Doyle. What is his relation to Sherlock Holmes? Give an oral report of your findings to the class.
8. Write a short biography of the famous mystery writer Agatha Christie.

Writing

9. Write the first chapter of your own mystery story.
10. Create a new character for *The Hound of the Baskervilles*. In a brief essay, write a dialogue for this character and explain how the character would fit into the story.

Miscellaneous

11. Complete the Character Attribute Web on page 13 of this guide for the character of your choice, excluding Sir Henry Baskerville.
12. Create three alternate titles for the novel.
13. Relate to the class a time when you were particularly afraid or felt as if you were in danger.

Assessment for *The Hound of the Baskervilles*

Assessment is an ongoing process. The following ten items can be completed during the novel study. Once finished, the student and teacher will check the work. Points may be added to indicate the level of understanding.

Name _____ Date _____

Student   **Teacher**

_____   _____   1. Complete the Understanding Values graphic on page 14 of this guide.

_____   _____   2. Check all quizzes and tests taken on the novel.

_____   _____   3. Write an alternate ending to the novel.

_____   _____   4. Compare your completed Prediction Charts and Story Maps in a small group.

_____   _____   5. View a Sherlock Holmes movie and compare his character in the movie to his character in *The Hound of the Baskervilles*.

_____   _____   6. Write a literary review of the novel for a newspaper in which you recommend the novel to other readers.

_____   _____   7. Write a diary entry that Miss Stapleton may have written after her husband's death.

_____   _____   8. Write a letter to Sherlock Holmes requesting his assistance with a mystery you are trying to solve.

_____   _____   9. Create a character sketch of Dr. Watson.

_____   _____   10. Create a collage of images, words, and feelings associated with the hound that haunts the Baskerville family.

Linking Novel Units® Lessons to National and State Reading Assessments

During the past several years, an increasing number of students have faced some form of state-mandated competency testing in reading. Many states now administer state-developed assessments to measure the skills and knowledge emphasized in their particular reading curriculum. The discussion questions and post-reading questions in this Novel Units® Teacher Guide make excellent open-ended comprehension questions and may be used throughout the daily lessons as practice activities. The rubric below provides important information for evaluating responses to open-ended comprehension questions. Teachers may also use scoring rubrics provided for their own state's competency test.

Please note: The Novel Units® Student Packet contains optional open-ended questions in a format similar to many national and state reading assessments.

Scoring Rubric for Open-Ended Items

3-Exemplary	Thorough, complete ideas/information Clear organization throughout Logical reasoning/conclusions Thorough understanding of reading task Accurate, complete response
2-Sufficient	Many relevant ideas/pieces of information Clear organization throughout most of response Minor problems in logical reasoning/conclusions General understanding of reading task Generally accurate and complete response
1-Partially Sufficient	Minimally relevant ideas/information Obvious gaps in organization Obvious problems in logical reasoning/conclusions Minimal understanding of reading task Inaccuracies/incomplete response
0-Insufficient	Irrelevant ideas/information No coherent organization Major problems in logical reasoning/conclusions Little or no understanding of reading task Generally inaccurate/incomplete response

Glossary

Chapters 1–3, pp. 9–45
1. ferrule (10): metal ring or cap placed around a shaft for reinforcement
2. erroneous (11): mistaken; incorrect
3. incredulously (13): skeptically; disbelieving
4. astutely (14): shrewdly; craftily
5. anthropological (16): the study of man's development
6. wanton (21): immoral; deliberate
7. leagues (22): a measure of distance by land (1 league ≈ 3 miles)
8. anon (23): soon; shortly
9. bemused (23): confused; bewildered
10. *roysterers (24): rioters; revelers
11. scion (26): descendant
12. prosaic (28): ordinary
13. chimerical (31): imaginary
14. diabolical (37): of, relating to, or characteristic of the devil
15. immaculate (41): spotless; clean and pure

*archaic spelling

Chapters 4–6, pp. 46–91
1. pugnacious (46): belligerent; quarrelsome
2. foolscap (47): piece of writing paper formerly used in Great Britain
3. bourgeois (50): marked by a tendency toward mediocrity
4. singular (53): peculiar; unusual
5. languid (57): lethargic, showing little energy
6. hansom (58): light, 2-wheeled covered carriage with the driver's seat elevated behind
7. malevolent (59): evil; spiteful
8. articulate (65): able to speak clearly or effectively
9. entailed (69): to assign or confer permanently
10. inexplicable (72): unexplainable
11. toff (76): a man who gives exaggerated attention to personal appearance
12. imprudent (80): unwise; lacking discretion
13. bracken (83): a large coarse fern
14. equestrian (83): representing a person on horseback
15. atrocious (84): appalling; revolting
16. surmounted (85): topped
17. crenellated (86): furnished with battlements for defense or decoration
18. mullioned (86): divided by vertical strips
19. balustraded (89): having a railing and supportive posts
20. resonant (90): echoing; intense

Chapters 7–9, pp. 92–144
1. pallid (93): pale; lacking sparkle or liveliness
2. propitious (94): advantageous; favorable
3. ruse (95): trick; plan intended to mislead
4. placid (98): unconcerned
5. wary (98): watchful; cautious
6. undulating (99): moving in a flowing or wavelike manner
7. mottled (101): spotty; blotched

8. wizened (106): aged; wrinkled
9. monoliths (112): massive stones
10. antiquarian (112): one who studies ancient people or times
11. disapprobation (115): disapproval
12. onerous (115): troublesome
13. choleric (116): easily angered; hot-tempered
14. effigy (117): publicly scorned
15. stealthy (119): secretly; deliberately; slowly
16. furtive (119): shifty; sly
17. peremptory (127): expressive of urgency or command
18. unmitigated (137): unchanging; absolute; definite
19. inscrutable (144): not readily understood; mysterious

Chapters 10–12, pp. 145–193
1. sodden (153): heavy with moisture
2. morass (153): marsh or swamp
3. equivocal (155): doubtful; uncertain
4. almoner (162): one who helps the needy
5. reticent (166): restrained; uncommunicative
6. roughshod (168): marked by tyrannical force
7. incredulity (170): the quality of being skeptical or doubtful
8. solicitations (172): persuasive arguments
9. dilapidated (173): decayed; ruined; in disrepair
10. pannikin (174): a small pan or cup
11. malignant (175): evil in nature, influence, or effect
12. tenacity (178): the quality of being persistent or strong
13. irrevocable (188): not capable of being altered or changed
14. precipitous (188): extremely steep
15. paroxysm (189): sudden outburst

Chapters 13–15, pp. 194–240
1. connoisseur (199): expert
2. implicitly (202): totally; without reservation
3. serrated (214): notched or toothed on the edge
4. exultant (216): expressing great joy or triumph
5. hackles (216): hairs that stand up on the neck and back; especially on a dog
6. mastiff (217): a massive, powerful breed of dog
7. doddering (219): trembling from weakness or age
8. swathed (220): bound; wrapped
9. dupe (221): fool
10. quagmires (222): soft, muddy areas that are easy to sink into
11. miasmatic (222): polluting; foggy
12. barrister (227): a lawyer in an English superior court
13. purloined (228): stolen
14. finesse (230): skill; refinement
15. specious (231): deceptive; alluring
16. expedient (233): suitable for achieving the desired results, but without regard for ethics or consequences
17. audacity (233): bold or arrogant disregard
18. elucidate (234): explain; clarify

Novel Units® Teacher Guides and Student Packets

64	NU6172SP	Man Who Was Poe, The
529	NU90536SP	Messenger
11	NU802XSP	Midwife's Apprentice, The
307	NU90314SP	Milkweed
31	NU5314SP	Miracle Worker, The
09	NU7217SP	Miracle's Boys
369	NU90376SP	Misfits, The
41		Moves Make the Man, The
30	NU5322SP	Mrs. Frisby and the Rats of NIMH
0X	NU8232SP	My Brother Sam Is Dead
25	NU7233SP	My Louisiana Sky
68	NU4946SP	My Side of the Mountain
61	NU9478SP	No More Dead Dogs
92		No Promises in the Wind
06		Nothing But the Truth
93	NU5907SP	Out of the Dust
21	NU4067SP	Outsiders, The
42	NU7950SP	Parrot in the Oven: Mi Vida
57	NU3265SP	Pearl, The
506	NU76667SP	Peter Pan
20	NU9139SP	Phoenix Rising
93	NU3907SP	Pigman, The
67	NU7675SP	Prince and the Pauper, The
284	NU90291SP	Red Kayak
07	NU4415SP	Red Pony, The
12	NU8620SP	Red Scarf Girl
83	NU7691SP	Redwall
844	NU75851SP	Rip Van Winkle and Other Stories
16		River, The
76	NU0283SP	Romiette and Julio
027	NU81034SP	Rules of the Road
24	NU9331SP	Running Out of Time
86	NU8194SP	Samurai's Tale, The
921	NU80938SP	Schooled
35		Scorpions
00	NU9317SP	Sea Wolf, The
71	NU0795SP	Seedfolks
26	NU6334SP	Shabanu: Daughter of the Wind
84		Shadow of a Bull
62	NU7470SP	Shiva's Fire
20	NU4954SP	Sign of the Beaver, The
945	NU80952SP	Silent to the Bone
47	NU9454SP	Skin I'm In, The
35		Slave Dancer, The
4X		Snow Bound
806	NU75813SP	So B. It
88	NU5796SP	So Far from the Bamboo Grove
09	NU9416SP	Soldier's Heart
59		Solitary Blue
468	NU90475SP	Somewhere in the Darkness
820	NU75837SP	Son of the Mob
06	NU4962SP	Sounder
4		Soup
68	NU7276SP	Space Station Seventh Grade
02	NU5710SP	Staying Fat for Sarah Byrnes
206	NU77213SP	Stormbreaker
14		Streams to the River, River to the Sea
22		Summer of Fear
30		Summer of My German Soldier
71	NU868XSP	Surviving the Applewhites
44	NU0375SP	Swallowing Stones
48	NU7756SP	Taking Sides
87	NU6695SP	Tangerine
09	NU6717SP	Tears of a Tiger
48	NU9355SP	Things Not Seen
55		Tiger Eyes
44	NU8852SP	Tiger, Tiger, Burning Bright
22		Timothy of the Cay
73	NU5281SP	Touching Spirit Bear
60	NU8879SP	Toughing It
93		Transport 7-41-R
43	NU7543SP	Treasure Island
61		Twenty-One Balloons, The
93	NU8507SP	20,000 Leagues Under the Sea
128	NU87135SP	Uglies
08	NU7716SP	Walk Two Moons
8X	NU9198SP	Warriors Don't Cry
166	NU87173SP	Wednesday Wars, The
43	NU8151SP	Weirdo, The
30	NU8038SP	West Against the Wind
44	NU4652SP	Westing Game, The
1X	NU8728SP	When My Name Was Keoko
29	NU4237SP	When the Legends Die
41	NU675XSP	When Zachary Beaver Came to Town
NU6342	NU6350SP	Where the Lilies Bloom
NU2447	NU4970SP	Where the Red Fern Grows
NU3362	NU5276SP	White Fang
NU8736	NU8744SP	Winterdance
NU2463	NU5349SP	Witch of Blackbird Pond, The
NU9201	NU921XSP	Witness
NU76094	NU76100SP	Wolf Rider
NU4172		Woodsong
NU1181	NU4989SP	Wrinkle in Time, A
NU8248	NU8256SP	Yearling, The
NU9423	NU9430SP	Young Fu of the Upper Yangtze
NU8887	NU8895SP	Z for Zachariah
NU7047	NU7055SP	Zlata's Diary: A Child's Life in Sarajevo

Grades 9–12

See a complete list of Grades 9–12 titles at novelunits.com.

NU1823	NU3087SP	Adventures of Huckleberry Finn, The
NU5500	NU5517SP	Alas, Babylon
NU90383	NU90390SP	Alchemist, The
NU6191	NU6205SP	All Quiet on the Western Front
NU9131	NU914XSP	All the Pretty Horses
NU75721	NU75738SP	Angela's Ashes
NU6180	NU6199SP	Animal Dreams
NU3052	NU3060SP	Animal Farm
NU7449	NU7457SP	Antigone
NU7802	NU7810SP	Around the World in 80 Days
NU5532	NU5540SP	As I Lay Dying
NU5047	NU5055SP	As You Like It
NU9584	NU9591SP	Autobiography of Miss Jane Pittman, The
NU756X	NU7578SP	Awakening, The
NU8909	NU8917SP	Bean Trees, The
NU8000	NU8019SP	Beowulf
NU9158	NU9166SP	Billy Budd
NU6202	NU6210SP	Black Boy
NU8062	NU8070SP	Bless Me, Ultima
NU708X	NU7098SP	Bluest Eye, The
NU9560	NU9577SP	Body of Christopher Creed, The
NU75769	NU75776SP	Book Thief, The
NU4458	NU4466SP	Brave New World
NU87203	NU87210SP	Bronx Masquerade
NU5063	NU5071SP	Cannery Row
NU9190	NU9204SP	Canterbury Tales, The
NU90543	NU90550SP	Catch-22
NU4490	NU4504SP	Catcher in the Rye, The
NU2064	NU6299SP	Chocolate War, The
NU7465	NU7473SP	Chosen, The
NU5913	NU5920SP	Chronicle of a Death Foretold
NU0504	NU0511SP	Cold Mountain
NU508X	NU5098SP	Cold Sassy Tree
NU7829	NU7837SP	Color of Water, The
NU5079	NU5087SP	Color Purple, The
NU75660	NU75677SP	Copper Sun
NU7128	NU7136SP	Count of Monte Cristo, The
NU8027	NU8035SP	Crime and Punishment
NU363X	NU3648SP	Crucible, The
NU3540	NU3559SP	Cry, the Beloved Country
NU90345	NU90352SP	Curious Incident of the Dog in the Night-Time, The
NU6213	NU6221SP	Cyrano de Bergerac
NU7481	NU749XSP	Dandelion Wine
NU5101	NU511XSP	David Copperfield
NU1491		Death Be Not Proud
NU1858	NU3850SP	Death of a Salesman
NU8925	NU8933SP	Doll's House, A/Hedda Gabler
NU6229	NU6237SP	Downriver
NU7845	NU7853SP	Dr. Jekyll and Mr. Hyde
NU6504	NU6512SP	Dracula
NU5095	NU5109SP	Edgar Allan Poe: A Collection of Stories
NU5128	NU5136SP	Ethan Frome
NU301X	NU3028SP	Fahrenheit 451
NU6369	NU6377SP	Fallen Angels
NU4547	NU4555SP	Farewell to Arms, A
NU806X	NU8078SP	Fellowship of the Ring, The
NU90123	NU90130SP	Fences
NU8531	NU854XSP	Five People You Meet in Heaven, The
NU7503	NU7511SP	Frankenstein
NU6865	NU6873SP	Gathering of Old Men, A
NU904X	NU9058SP	Gift of the Magi and Other Stories, The
NU1866	NU3370SP	Glass Menagerie, The
NU6520	NU6539SP	Good Earth, The
NU2994	NU3001SP	Grapes of Wrath, The
NU5144	NU5152SP	Great Expectations
NU3168	NU3176SP	Great Gatsby, The
NU75608	NU75615SP	Grendel
NU9212	NU9220SP	Gulliver's Travels
NU4180	NU4199SP	Hamlet
NU0719	NU0726SP	Handmaid's Tale, The
NU3729	NU3737SP	Heart is a Lonely Hunter, The
NU6245	NU6253SP	Heart of Darkness/ Secret Sharer, The
NU136X		Hiroshima
NU8558	NU8566SP	Hound of the Baskervilles, The
NU9546	NU9553SP	House of the Scorpion, The
NU8981	NU899XSP	House of the Seven Gables, The
NU4830	NU5591SP	House on Mango Street, The
NU9607	NU9614SP	How the García Girls Lost Their Accents
NU8574	NU8582SP	Hunchback of Notre Dame, The
NU4849	NU6345SP	I Know Why the Caged Bird Sings
NU752X	NU7538SP	Iliad, The
NU87326	NU87333SP	In Cold Blood
NU658X	NU6598SP	Inferno
NU6601	NU661XSP	Inherit the Wind
NU87227	NU87234SP	Into the Wild
NU81126	NU81133SP	Invisible Man
NU5605	NU5613SP	Ironman
NU7546	NU7554SP	Ishi, Last of His Tribe
NU4628	NU4636SP	Jane Eyre
NU8941	NU895XSP	Joy Luck Club, The
NU3036	NU3044SP	Julius Caesar
NU9007	NU9015SP	Jungle, The
NU75509	NU73826SP	Kaffir Boy
NU9239	NU9247SP	King Lear
NU90482	NU90499SP	Kite Runner, The
NU6628	NU6636SP	Last of the Mohicans, The
NU7562	NU7570SP	Les Misérables
NU742X	NU7438SP	Lesson Before Dying, A
NU81102	NU81119SP	Life of Pi
NU90567	NU90574SP	Like Water for Chocolate
NU7187	NU7195SP	Little Prince, The
NU5648	NU5656SP	Long Day's Journey Into Night
NU3834	NU3842SP	Lord of the Flies
NU4369	NU4377SP	Macbeth
NU5745	NU5753SP	Madame Bovary
NU8825	NU8833SP	Malcolm X: By Any Means Necessary
NU81164	NU81171SP	Marley & Me: Life and Love with the World's Worst Dog
NU7926	NU7934SP	Martian Chronicles, The
NU81225	NU81232SP	Maus I: My Father Bleeds History
NU3508	NU3516SP	Mayor of Casterbridge, The
NU5664	NU5672SP	Merchant of Venice, The
NU7446	NU7454SP	Metamorphosis, The
NU5187	NU5195SP	Midsummer Night's Dream, A
NU6881	NU689XSP	Monster
NU9255	NU9263SP	Much Ado About Nothing
NU75646	NU75653SP	Murder on the Orient Express
NU7589	NU7597SP	My Ántonia
NU816X	NU8178SP	Mythology
NU413X	NU4148SP	1984
NU623X	NU6248SP	Native Son
NU8046	NU8054SP	Night
NU8167	NU8175SP	October Sky
NU7600	NU7619SP	Odyssey, The
NU7627	NU7635SP	Oedipus the King
NU1874	NU3109SP	Of Mice and Men
NU4032	NU4040SP	Old Man and the Sea, The
NU9066	NU9074SP	Oliver Twist
NU7640	NU7659SP	Once and Future King, The
NU8396	NU840XSP	One Flew Over the Cuckoo's Nest
NU90246	NU90253SP	Ordinary People
NU5209	NU5217SP	Othello
NU6256	NU6264SP	Our Town
NU81188	NU81195SP	Peace Like A River
NU81201	NU81218SP	Persepolis: The Story of a Childhood
NU7241	NU725XSP	Picture of Dorian Gray, The
NU75684	NU75691SP	Poisonwood Bible, The
NU7643	NU7651SP	Portrait of the Artist as a Young Man, A
NU766X	NU7678SP	Pride and Prejudice
NU75707	NU75714SP	Princess Bride, The
NU9271	NU928XSP	Pygmalion
NU3125	NU3133SP	Raisin in the Sun, A
NU6660	NU6679SP	Rebecca
NU346X	NU3478SP	Red Badge of Courage, The
NU87289	NU87296SP	Road, The
NU3745	NU3753SP	Romeo and Juliet
NU9147	NU9155SP	Rosencrantz & Guildenstern are Dead
NU1440		Rumble Fish
NU3389	NU3397SP	Scarlet Letter, The
NU6385	NU6393SP	Scarlet Pimpernel, The
NU0245	NU0252SP	Secret Life of Bees, The
NU8968	NU8976SP	Sense and Sensibility
NU3990	NU4008SP	Separate Peace, A
NU2773	NU5330SP	Shane
NU6946	NU6954SP	Siddhartha
NU6407	NU6415SP	Slam!
NU7500	NU7519SP	Slaughterhouse-Five
NU5842	NU5850SP	Snow Falling on Cedars
NU87302	NU87319SP	Something Wicked This Way Comes
NU8828	NU8836SP	Song of Be
NU9379	NU9387SP	Song of Solomon
NU6989	NU6997SP	Speak
NU7721	NU773XSP	Step from Heaven, A
NU9298	NU9301SP	Stranger, The
NU9508	NU9515SP	Streetcar Named Desire, A
NU90260	NU90277SP	Sula
NU8205	NU8213SP	Sun Also Rises, The
NU4326	NU4334SP	Tale of Two Cities, A
NU7686	NU7694SP	Taming of the Shrew, The
NU6272	NU6280SP	Tempest, The
NU4261	NU427XSP	Tess of the D'Urbervilles
NU1467		Tex
NU5225	NU5233SP	That Was Then, This Is Now
NU8089	NU8097SP	Their Eyes Were Watching God
NU8127	NU8135SP	Things Fall Apart
NU7969	NU7977SP	Things They Carried, The
NU81089	NU81096SP	Thousand Splendid Suns, A
NU7004	NU7012SP	Three Musketeers, The
NU5257	NU5265SP	Time Machine, The
NU1572	NU3079SP	To Kill a Mockingbird
NU9522	NU9539SP	Tree Grows in Brooklyn, A
NU8450	NU8469SP	Tuesdays with Morrie
NU931X	NU9328SP	Turn of the Screw, The
NU5869	NU5877SP	Twelfth Night
NU90628	NU90635SP	Twelve Angry Men
NU81140	NU81157SP	Twilight
NU8698	NU8701SP	Uncle Tom's Cabin
NU87265	NU87272SP	Unwind
NU0887	NU0900SP	Walk in the Woods, A
NU7020	NU7039SP	War of the Worlds, The
NU6423	NU6431SP	Watership Down
NU6725	NU6733SP	Wave, The
NU75622	NU75639SP	We Beat the Street
NU9621	NU9638SP	When I Was Puerto Rican
NU4598	NU4601SP	Wuthering Heights
NU9336	NU9344SP	Yellow Raft in Blue Water, A

Additional Products

NU783XRH		Graphic Organizer Collection

Award Winners

For a complete list of titles that have won major awards, including the Newbery Honor, the Coretta Scott King Award, the Pulitzer Prize, and the National Book Award, see our catalog or Web site.

Newbery Medal Winners

NU8752	NU8760SP	Adam of the Road
NU5052	NU5060SP	Amos Fortune: Free Man
NU248X	NU4881SP	Bridge to Terabithia
NU2552		Caddie Woodlawn
NU8043	NU8051SP	Crispin: The Cross of Lead
NU6183	NU7171SP	Giver, The
NU90604	NU90611SP	Good Masters! Sweet Ladies!
NU73666	NU73673SP	Graveyard Book, The
NU0542	NU0566SP	Higher Power of Lucky, The
NU6148	NU6156SP	Holes
NU2528	NU489XSP	Island of the Blue Dolphins
NU1017		It's Like This, Cat
NU1262	NU8364SP	Jacob Have I Loved
NU9228	NU9236SP	Kira-Kira
NU1149	NU8313SP	Summer of the Swans, The
NU5230	NU5249SP	Tale of Despereaux, The
NU3761		Twenty-One Balloons, The
NU81249	NU81256SP	When You Reach Me
NU0894	NU7112SP	Whipping Boy, The

Caldecott Medal Winners

NU81065	NU81072SP	Invention of Hugo Cabret, The
NU4733		Madeline's Rescue
NU2307		Make Way for Ducklings
NU1963		Polar Express, The
NU0223		Where the Wild Things Are
NU4784		Why Mosquitoes Buzz in People's Ears

ndicates Student Packet for this title.

se contact us if you do not see the title you are looking for. We are always adding new titles.

NU8558

Novel Units® Teacher Guides and Student Packets

Great Alone, Phenomenal in Tandem

It's like buying time!℠

No content overlaps in matching Teacher Guide and Student Packet.

Created by teachers for teachers
All the tools you need to teach a novel
All the books you want to teach...and students want to read

Each Teacher Guide includes:

- Summary
- "About the Author"
- Character list
- Background information
- Initiating activities
- Vocabulary activities
- Discussion questions and answers
- Graphic organizers
- Writing ideas
- Literary analysis
- Post-reading discussion
- Cross-curriculum extension activities
- Assessment
- Scoring rubric
- Glossary (Gr. 9–12)

Each Student Packet includes:

Activities and assessments are tagged with skills/objectives.

- Prereading activities
- Vocabulary activities
- Study guide
- Graphic organizers
- Literary analysis
- Character analysis
- Writing activities
- Critical- and creative-thinking challenges
- Comprehension quizzes
- Unit test
- Answer key
- Scoring rubric

Student Packet Value Packs

Now you can provide a Student Packet to each child. Consumable versions of Student Packets are available in bundles of 15 or 30 at special prices.

We have the largest selection of literature guides.
Hundreds of Novel Units® titles to choose from!

ISBN 1-58130-855-8